# Pythagorean Healing
## Level One

Shelley A. Kaehr, Ph.D.

Copyright © 2019 Shelley A. Kaehr, Ph.D. *Pythagorean Healing: Level One* ©2019
All Rights Reserved.
Cover design by Shelley Kaehr
Chakra charts & number images by Shelley Kaehr

Graphic images procured from Canva.com

*Products and services are not intended to diagnose, treat, cure, or prevent any disease. Always check with a medical professional for your health concerns. By accessing and using this website and its related goods, services, and other connected sites, links, and resources, you agree and accept that Shelley A. Kaehr and any other party involved with creation or management of this site is not liable for any damage or loss in any form arising out of your access or use of this site and its related content and services. You accept all responsibility for your interpretations, decisions, uses, actions, and consequences resulting from your access to this site and its related content in all forms.*

To My Readers:
Know that the universe is a wondrous place and energy medicine is an integral part of my life that I believe in with every fiber of my being. That said, while energy healing can bring real peace to body, mind and spirit, it cannot replace medical care or good old fashioned common sense. Should you require medical attention, please seek out a professional. My books are not designed to replace the medical or psychiatric communities, and while I do believe in what I teach, I make no claims about any specific results you may or may not receive from practicing these techniques. Each soul is a complex combustion of energy and information from past lives, paths we agreed to experience before we incarnated, lessons and learnings we hope to obtain, and so forth. What works for one won't work the same for another. I do hope that this material will help you in a way that will be most for your Highest Good and that whatever form that takes brings you greater peace in life.
Sending You Joy & Happiness on Your Path,
Dr. Shelley
www.pastlifelady.com
ISBN: 9781695465541

## DEDICATION
To All Seekers.
May you find happiness in your life.

### Visit Dr. Shelley online:
www.pastlifelady.com
YouTube Channel: Past Life Lady
Facebook Fan Pages: Past Life Lady,
Shelley Kaehr
Instagram: shelleykaehr
Twitter: @shelleykaehr

### Also by Shelley A. Kaehr, Ph.D.:
*Edgar Cayce's Egyptian Energy Healing*
*Edgar Cayce's Guide to Gemstones, Minerals, Metals & More*
*Edgar Cayce's Sacred Stones*
*Holographic Mapping: Energy Healing Made Simple*
*Binary Healing: Pythagorean Healing Level Two*
*Platonic Healing: Pythagorean Healing Level Three*
*Galactic Healing*
*Lemurian Seeds: Hope for Humanity*

For a full list of Shelley's books, visit her Amazon.com author page.

www.pastlifelady.com

# CONTENTS

|   | Introduction | 1 |
|---|---|---|
| 1 | Why This? Why Now? | 6 |
| 2 | Healing vs. Numerology Numbers | 9 |
| 3 | The Primary Numbers | 16 |
| 4 | How to Use Numbers for Healing | 28 |
| 5 | Self-Healing with Primary Numbers | 32 |
| 6 | Healing Others with Primary Numbers | 41 |
| 7 | Distance Healing with Primary Numbers | 52 |
| 8 | Group Healing with Primary Numbers | 54 |
|   | Conclusion | 57 |
|   | Website Resources | 59 |
|   | About the Author | 60 |

# INTRODUCTION

This is the first book in a series of techniques I collectively call **Pythagorean Healing**. Pythagoras was a Greek philosopher and founder of a movement called Pythagoreanism. He was known for developing theories about mathematics, numbers, music and the sacred geometrical foundations that make up all things in the known universe.

What you're about to experience is an incredibly powerful and simultaneously simple numbers based method for clearing your energy field that will help you bring more peace to body, mind and spirit. Although I am a huge fan of numerology and I do believe that numbers are important energetically in terms of shifting our fortunes and determining various things about our life plans, this book is *not about numerology*. Instead, we will use the primary numbers as energy healing symbols.

Incredibly, this information first came to me back in the early 2000's, and although I considered publishing the process back then, I was clearly guided to wait. I do recall showing a version of the number chart you'll see later in the book to a few of my students, but the idea never caught on. Over the years, I've pulled this information out of my drawer and worked with it and I've considered publishing it several other times, but over and over again, I felt guided to continue waiting, but to keep the material in the files for some future date.

Recently after my book *Edgar Cayce's Egyptian Energy Healing* was released and I began working with that new modality, I was guided that now is the time to finally publish this new and simple way of doing energy healing because ECEEH (the acronym for Edgar Cayce's Egyptian Energy Healing) and all of the techniques in my new Pythagorean Healing series are energetically similar in terms of how the methods are introduced into the energy field. Both are extraordinarily simple, and simultaneously advanced in the way they perform and the things they can do. During a recent ECEEH class, I presented this material alongside that technique and continue to do so, as the students found them so helpful.

The technique I will present in *Pythagorean Healing* is not at all like Reiki or the other modalities I developed, Holographic Mapping and Galactic Healing, or any other of the many courses I've taken over the years. Instead of working on the energetic fields around the physical body, the various levels of Pythagorean Healing are delivered in line with the new energy that's coming into our planet at this time.

The things you've learned before about how energy healing works – even from me if you've read any of my other books over the years – must be shifted to a new way of thinking in order to use this method. Rather than working on Etheric fields which are energies that surround our physical bodies, Pythagorean Healing will shift the body at the cellular and DNA level and the Etheric fields will be impacted as a result of these internal shifts. Reiki and other modalities work to enliven the exterior fields around the body to create interior healing, but each of the Pythagorean techniques are the exact opposite. The energy travels down through the crown of the head, through the spine and limbs and out the soles of the feet with the ending result being an expansion of the Etheric fields from the inside out.

In my earlier *Galactic Healing* book, the actual symbols were never publically released, and I am guided at this point, that although that writing offers my first attempt to channel the alien being who shared the information with me, the way we do energy healing needs to change and that information will be updated through this new modality. First off, all the material will be presented in its entirety throughout the books so by the time you read each one, you will know the various symbols and be able to do everything I am talking about without having to travel anywhere or take an expensive class, be it in person or online. If you choose to study with me personally, so be it, but it will not be required to access this information. I am a huge believer that this information needs to get out to as many people who want to receive it at a price people can afford. We don't have time to waste!

Pythagorean Healing will involve several easy-to-do steps that represent the new way, the latest techniques, for how energy healing should be performed at this moment in history. If you've found this book, congratulations! You're ready for a cellular upgrade into the next chapter of human development. Let's get started!

Pythagoras

# CHAPTER ONE
# WHY THIS? WHY NOW?

By now, I think many of us in the spiritual community thought some supersonic shift would happen to us in the year 2000 with the Y2K craze. Also back in 2012, because the Mayan calendar was ending, everyone thought that the lights would turn off and back on again, and we would be reborn into some utopian bliss where we were living peacefully amongst one another and there would be no further challenges to face, ever again. Am I right?

Well folks, guess what? That didn't quite go as planned. Many metaphysical people are sadly disappointed with what seems to be our lack of progress and *devolvement* into behaviors we all hoped we'd outgrown. With all this turmoil spinning around, there's also a ton of wonderful things happening. Overall, I still believe we're moving and shifting energies so rapidly, that things are still going in the right direction, despite what's going on in the outer world. We must have faith and hang in there!

    These new energies that are coming in are here to help us to alter our physical bodies to be in alignment with the ever-shifting frequencies around our planet. Things are not the same as they were back in the 2000's. They're not the same as they were two months ago, and by the time you get this book downloaded into your phone, the world will be changed yet again.

    Several years ago I wrote a book called *Holographic Mapping* where you do incredibly easy clearing processes on the Etheric fields around the physical body. It may sound strange, but I write so many books, that I had literally forgotten about this technique until I taught it to a group earlier this year. The students were eager to learn and told me how much they loved the simplicity of the method. I feel guided to remind folks about that one too because simple is better. Easy is okay. I will include a list of these other books in here so you can go check those out if you're guided.

    *Pythagorean Healing* books will be divided into levels with one procedure per level. I'm guided to inform you that for best results, the techniques should be used in the order they are written. Once you get used to doing them, in the end, it's up to you how you choose to do this. Each method does deep clearings and once you try them, if you're like me, you will probably find one you like the best, and you'll use your favorite more than the others. That works! Take the best, leave the rest, as they say.

You may also want to return to the information periodically because during different times in our lives, various ideas and ways of doing things resonate better than others. After working as a healer for many years and training thousands of students, I began working with primary numbers years ago and found that they offer some of the best healing energy you can ever find.

Overall, I am happy to finally be able to share this with you and I hope you enjoy the processes. My goal is to help you find tools you can use to create more peace, happiness and balance in your life. With that, let's take a look at the first level of *Pythagorean Healing* working with the primary numbers. Enjoy!

# CHAPTER TWO
# HEALING VS. NUMEROLOGY NUMBERS

This is not a numerology book. That said, I felt it necessary to include a brief description of basic numerology to demonstrate the differences between using numbers for healing verses how they're used in the science of numerology.

For those of you who are familiar with traditional numerology, numbers are traditionally listed as:

| | | |
|---|---|---|
| 1 = | Red = | AJS |
| 2 = | Orange = | BKT |
| 3 = | Yellow = | CLU |
| 4 = | Green = | DMV |
| 5 = | Blue = | ENW |
| 6 = | Indigo | FOX |
| 7 = | Violet = | GPY |
| 8 = | Rose = | HQZ |
| 9 = | Gold = | IR |

You can use the system above to calculate your name to see what number you vibrate or resonate to. Like a good astrology reading, the information can tell you a lot about your personality and various things you will meet on the path of life.

For example, let's look at my first name:

S – H – E – L – L – E - Y

To add up my name, we would use the following:
S = 1
H = 8
E = 5
L = 3
L = 3
E = 5
Y = 7
Total = 32
3 + 2 = 5

This means my name is vibrating to the frequency of the number 5.

Although I told you this is not a numerology book, in my personal interpretation, the primary numbers in numerology are attributed to the following traits:

1 = the self
2 = partnership
3 = creativity
4 = the home
5 = energy
6 = health
7 = spirituality
8 = prosperity
9 = completion

There are many awesome websites you can turn to with free numerology calculators and people who have been studying this professionally for years.

For me, numerology is kind of like Feng Shui. I love it and yet I get confused listening to so many sources, so I finally found one book I love and I use that one consistently for all things Feng Shui.

The Runes are the same. I have one book I've been using for years so that my guides understand how I am interpreting various things and they can communicate better with me.

When it comes to numerology though, I don't use one particular source. I simply go to the net and see what resonates. There are tons of free resources out there if you check, so please keep in mind that the above interpretation of numbers may not follow exactly what you've heard from others, but it's my personal take on numerological meanings of our primary numbers.

For this project, I'm not concerned with numerology, but how we are going to use these ancient symbols in healing. First, let's look at the chakras.

## Seven Traditional Chakra Numbers

One of the interesting aspects to the assignment of colors on many numerology charts is that they tend to follow along the lines of the seven primary chakra centers that we've come to understand over the past several years, the ones I've been teaching in my many books on gem and mineral healing. Here they are for your reference:

Red = Root Chakra = 1
Orange – Sacral Chakra = 2
Yellow = Solar Plexus Chakra = 3
Green = Heart Chakra = 4
Blue = Throat Chakra = 5
Indigo = Third Eye Chakra = 6
Violet = Crown Chakra = 7

*Pythagorean Healing*

# Chakras

It is widely known that there are far more than seven chakras within and around the physical body. We are truly infinite beings and I don't think we know all the magnificent abilities and powers we actually have at our disposal. If we could see ourselves with the same unconditional love and far reaching loving kindness our creator views us, I think we'd be blown away. If learning energy healing does nothing else for you, I pray it opens you up to the light of your true magnificence.

In addition to our many colored light

centers, we also have infinite fields of light within and around us too. I'll talk more about the Etheric fields later in the book, but suffice to say, you're more amazing than you might think. Plus, because energies are shifting quickly around the planet and vibrations are rising, everything we've come to know about our universe is in a complete state of flux, and that includes the colors of our chakras.

When you look at the colors assigned to the numbers in the following pages, you should note that they are *not the same* colors as what we've been taught to use in the past to represent our primary chakra centers.

Did I mention we need to view Pythagorean Healing with an open mind and realize that nothing we've come to understand in the past is necessarily how things will continue to be in the future? Well, it's true.

In fact, I was so set on wanting my book to feature these same traditional numbers with the colors used from the past, that in an early incarnation of this book, I tried changing the colors to the ones listed above, and was clearly guided later on to stop doing that. The numbers I originally channeled about 20 years ago were brought through in the correct way *for this time in history*, and those colors should not be changed. Message received! I mention this so you won't question why they don't match. I've used them so long now and the results speak for themselves.

I believe this is a forebear to new information that will come in soon as to what these new chakras are doing and the fact that since they are new vibrations, and vibrations create color, we should expect the vibes, and subsequently the colors, to be different than what we've seen and done in the past.

I had a similar experience when learning to work with ECEEH (Edgar Cayce's Egyptian Energy Healing). I wanted the 9 symbols to relate to the old chakra system so it would be "easy" for me to explain to people, but I soon realized that they were not at all like anything else I'd (or my students) had ever worked with before. The symbols are fast acting, as are the numbers, and they are in their own alignment for what's yet to come. Ready to see what they are and try this? Great! Let's get started!

# CHAPTER THREE
# THE PRIMARY NUMBERS

Our environment is in constant flux. The only thing we can do is learn to be more flexible in our energy, attitudes and physical selves to keep up with the changes that will continue to go on as long as we're in our earth bodies.

The techniques you will read about in the *Pythagorean Healing* series are incredibly simple, yet they are simultaneously super charged and powerful in terms of rapidly upgrading the vibrational bodies into the new energy on earth. The simplicity is what I love most about the techniques. We humans tend to make everything about a thousand times more complex than they need to be. Simple is often more advanced, so just know that although the method is easy, it works.

Unlike most healing courses you've taken where the symbols are saved until the very end, we're going to start our journey by taking a look at our symbols, the numbers.

I will describe what each primary number represents in terms of using them in this healing modality and I'll share the color frequencies they present when working at their most effective state during the energy healing process. So using these numbers with the assigned colors I am putting forth here will create an initial shift that will help us all to be prepared for bigger changes down the road. If that resonates with you, so be it. Go for it. If not, that's fine too.

If you don't want to visualize the numbers in this chapter, or you have challenges with remembering the colors, another way to use the numbers in healing is to simply allow the numbers to move through the field without consciously recalling what colors I am mentioning here at all. Just imagine the numbers one through nine and ask that they be delivered for your highest good. Our Higher Self and guides work out the details.

Ready? Let's check them out!

Shelley A. Kaehr, Ph.D.

# ONE
## Peace
## Color: Violet

One represents peace, unity and wholeness. To best utilize its energy, imagine the number 1 in your mind's eye and feel it opening your crown chakra and swiftly moving down to the base of the spine, opening and connecting you to the all that is and Source.
One is violet.

# TWO
## Protection
## Color: Yellow

Two is a protective energy and is used to create a shield around your physical body. Imagine two swirling up from the ground toward the head in a counter-clockwise direction, surrounding you in light, protecting body, mind & spirit. Two is a golden yellow color.

Shelley A. Kaehr, Ph.D.

# THREE
## Healing
## Color: Green
The healing energy of the number three repairs and restores the body, mind and spirit. Imagine three as a beautiful plant with long leaves growing and surrounding you. Three is green in color.

*Pythagorean Healing*

# FOUR
## Grounding
## Color: Red

Four activates the root chakra, the color red. You can feel four at the base of your spine. Imagine four moving from the top of your head, down your spine and down through the legs and out the soles of your feet, firmly planting you on the ground. Four is red.

Shelley A. Kaehr, Ph.D.

# FIVE
## Energy
## Color: Blue

Five brings energy and physical stamina to you. Five creates a state of abundance and heightened wellbeing and activates the emotional body, clearing heavier energy and bringing positivity into your life. Five is blue.

*Pythagorean Healing*

# SIX
## Creativity
## Color: Orange

Six stimulates creative flow, and assists in cellular regeneration. Six is used to recreate the cells into healthy wholeness and perfection. Allow the six to travel into every cell in the body, realigning in a state of perfect balance, peace and happiness. Six is orange.

Shelley A. Kaehr, Ph.D.

# SEVEN

## Love
## Color: Pink

Seven enlivens the heart center, opening and healing the emotional heart and physically restoring the heart, while aiding higher realms of spirituality. Seven moves through the heart, expanding circulation and sending love throughout the physical body and into the world at large. Seven is pink.

*Pythagorean Healing*

# EIGHT
**Infinity**
**Color: Aqua**
Eight travels through all chakras opening body, mind and spirit to the universal source. Eight circulates clockwise from the top of the head to the feet. Removing illusions, eight connects you to the infinite, lifts frequencies to new levels. Expand your consciousness into the infinite light of aqua colored eight.

Shelley A. Kaehr, Ph.D.

# NINE
## Completion
## Color: Silver

Nine brings completion and wholeness to healing, & solves problems. Need to make a decision about something? Wondering what your best course of action should be? Meditate on the nine to achieve resolution with highest purpose in mind. Nine is metallic silver colored.

*Pythagorean Healing*

# ZERO
## Source
## Color: Gold

Use zero as a protective shield at the end of healing to seal and maintain the integrity of your work. Gold connects you to Source, the All-That-Is, the infinite. Allow the zero to expand your field into a calm, centered state of spiritual peace, feeling oneness with all beings.

# CHAPTER FOUR
# HOW TO USE NUMBERS FOR HEALING

Many modalities, including this one, use different symbols to represent different states of being. Symbols in healing are nothing more than pictorial shortcuts to represent your intention. In modern terms, we use symbols daily. Have you pulled out your cell phone lately and sent an Emoji? Of course you have! Emojis are great examples of symbols.

You may be initiated into Reiki, the Japanese modality, which uses symbols to transmit healing. This modality is no different, except for here, instead of using the Reiki symbols, you will use the numbers as symbols instead.

Numbers are foundational to many things on our planet. Computers run based on numbers, nature can be better understood through mathematics.

Personally I was terrible at math in school, but guess what? That doesn't matter. In this case, you are going to use the energy of the numbers to help align the body into a state of perfection.

Before you do that though, there's something you will do first when using Pythagorean Healing.

The newer healing processes such as the ECEEH and Pythagorean Healing both utilize a set of symbols. Unlike other modalities I've used such as Reiki, to get the best results, you would need to send all the symbols (in this system, that's the primary numbers) to yourself and others as a whole set first and then you would go back a second time to tune in deeper and resolve any residual issues using specific symbols as you are guided.

For example, let's say you were doing a self healing and you had a sore knee. Of course you would want to do a healing on your knee, and with Pythagorean Healing in this level, you would send numbers one through nine in order through the crown or top of your head first, then you would go back a second time and send the numbers specifically to your knee.

Why would we need to send all the numbers together as a unit? In these newer 21st century healing methods, consciously knowing and understanding each and every thing that the individual symbol represents is not as important as working with the systems as a whole. In the past, you would use a symbol and perhaps you would skip others, but in Pythagorean Healing Level One and other techniques you are going to learn in higher levels of this modality, each number is an important part of a whole and you really don't have to know how or why it's working for you as long as you send all the numbers as a collective unit through the body.

In the example of your sore knee, once you send all the numbers through the crown, they travel down into the body, shifting, realigning, and straightening out the energy. Which specific number would do the best job? Over the years I've discovered there's no real way to know that answer for sure until the symbols are delivered. What works for one person does not work as well for another because we all have so many multidimensional layers to ourselves that determine our healing path. Our ability to heal and straighten up our light bodies is dependent upon lots of things including:

Pythagorean Healing

- Our Past Lives
- Our Karma
- Our Soul Contracts
- Life Lessons we determined to experience before we arrived in our current lifetime
- And so on…..

All energy healing involves your ability to use your imagination, so all you'll do is imagine these numbers are moving down from the top of your head, into your neck, shoulders, arms, hands, fingers, then moving down your spine, into your legs and feet.

You will send the numbers in order, one at a time, from 1 to 9. Then we will do something different once you reach the zero.

As with any energy healing modality, the goal is to alleviate blockages in each of the energetic layers, clear the chakra centers and set the intent that the person is in a state of balance and good health.

I am a huge believer in the fact that you cannot help anybody until you've worked on yourself, so like any good method, the first thing we will learn to do is self-healing.

# CHAPTER FIVE
# SELF-HEALING WITH PRIMARY NUMBERS

Before you ever attempt to work on others, you should do a self healing first to clear out your own energy and become the best version of yourself you can be at this moment in order to assist others.

Go ahead and send all the numbers through the top of your head, or crown chakra. How do you do this? Hold the following list in front of you, and then imagine each one of these colored numbers is floating down through the top of your head, down your arms, hands, fingers, through your spine, legs and into your feet. We are not going to use the zero yet, so for now, use the numbers 1 through 9 only. Imagine them in this order:

**1-Peace**
**2-Protection**
**3-Healing**
**4-Grounding**
**5-Energy**
**6-Creativity**
**7-Heart**
**8-Infinity**
**9-Completion**

    Once you do this, in terms of the old way energy healing was taught, it's like you've just given yourself an attunement. The difference is that rather than waiting for your guru to help you, the activation is something you've given to yourself. That's the new way!

    If you're like me and you are super sensitive, you may feel the different energies of the numbers as they move individually through the body, shifting, straightening and realigning your mind, body and spirit.

    If you are not as sensitive to feelings, that's okay too. You may not feel a thing. You may see colored lights or just have an inner knowing that the numbers are moving into the body to assist various cells in aligning you to a state of happiness, health, balance and vitality.

The imagination is the key. When you accept that the numbers are assisting you and you understand that how they're doing that may be outside your conscious awareness, you surrender and simply know that whatever is for your highest good is happening. Channeling the numbers through the body gets you in touch with your Higher Self, which is your soul, the part of you who is infinite and all-knowing. Tap into the person you are when you are out in between lives and you understand how this universe works and how things should be accomplished. Get in touch with the part of you that holds infinite universal wisdom. Know that the numbers are helping you and that all is well, and be okay with not necessarily understanding how that help is happening. Just know the energetic shift is for your highest good.

Then again, you may sense shifts and the numbers may cause various pictures, thoughts, feelings, old memories from the past to surface. If that happens, allow those images to pass through your mind and go away, knowing these things are getting healed and resolved.

Another way to do this is to notice if any memories or thoughts surface, and if they represent something that needs healing. If needed, imagine a cord of light connecting you with the thought or memory and cut the cord. Once that cord is disconnected, imagine a golden beam of light heals everything involved with this situation and allow the light to transform you until the energy shifts into either a positive state, or a more neutral state.

For more details on how to do a cord cutting, you can read about it in several of my other books or go to my YouTube channel, Past Life Lady, where I do a cord cutting demonstration. Cord cutting is incredibly powerful!

**Healing to the Torso & Other Areas**
Once you send the numbers 1 to 9 through the top of the head, then you may want to do more by sending them into the body on a more physical level by moving them through the center of the body.

To do that, just lie down and place your hands a couple inches from your body or you may place your hands on your stomach and imagine the numbers and the colored energies coming from your hands into your body and energy field.

Again, you can either consciously know what each number is doing, or you can just send whichever numbers you think you need at this time and notice how they make you feel. Open your mind and imagination to know which numbers need to be sent to specific parts of the body.

You may want to look at the numbers as you do this so you can see what colors they are, but remember, that is not necessarily important. Your intention is what matters most. So long as you ask your Higher Self to step in, the numbers will be received in the proper way and in the proper color regardless of whether or not your conscious mind can remember what those colors are. Just allow the numbers to move into the body and notice what you notice, but more important than any physical sensation is to believe and accept that they are assisting you in becoming more balanced.

Regarding the earlier example about the knee, now's the time to go ahead and also send the numbers into any other area that you believe needs work. Know that they are doing what they need to do as a whole unit, and if you happen to have one number pop into your mind's eye, go ahead and send that! It means your Higher Self is communicating with you and that's perfect! Always follow your own inner guidance no matter what.

Next, we will add our final step with the zero.

### Adding the Zero

Now you need to add in your golden zero. How will you do that? Super easily!

So you've already sent the primary numbers 1 through 9 through the top of your head, and maybe you took that a step further by sending them also through the torso or into any other area that needs healing(but again, that is not necessary unless you feel guided).

Once that's done, you end this section of your work by imagining the golden zero is floating above the top of your head.

# 0-Source

See the zero in your imagination, hovering over your head, and then imagine it is big like an inflatable donut you'd float on in a swimming pool. Visualize it moving down over your physical shell, surrounding you, hugging the body only an inch away from your physical self as it works its way down from the top of your head toward the soles of your feet.

Imagine this golden circle of light is moving over your physical shell, creating a protective layer of light that will stay with you. Once it reaches your feet, imagine it moves back up toward the top of your head. Once it's back to your head, it moves down to your feet again, up and down, up and down, again and again, washing over the field, carrying away unwanted influences while strengthening the shell around your body. Allow this to go on as long as you feel guided.

In my presentations, I like to show a photo of how I see this in my mind's eye. Did you ever watch the old Star Trek shows with the fabulous William Shatner? I loved those programs when I was growing up! They're still awesome, even now, despite the fact that our technological abilities for special effects filming are so much more advanced than they used to be.

On *Star Trek*, the crew of the Starship Enterprise would stand in the transporter and beam down to various planets. Right before they left the ship, a circle of bright white light surrounded their bodies before they dematerialized and reemerged on whatever planet they were visiting at the time.

For whatever reason (perhaps because the image makes me laugh) I see this golden zero donut like the transporters. You can do the same if that helps, or come up with your own way to imagine yourself being encircled by a bright light. Use whatever imagery that works for you. I do know that the *zero shield*, as I call it, does help tremendously with reinforcing the field around the body.

Sensitive people are often negatively impacted by the energies of their environments, so this zero, when used as a protective shield, will clear out those unwanted vibes and shield you against anything that is not for your highest and best.

This is super easy to do, and makes me feel stronger and more prepared to face the challenges of the day.

Try it and I think you'll agree!

### Other Considerations

Earlier I mentioned that you can do self healing lying down. If that's not possible, you can also just sit in a chair and send the numbers into your field by placing your hands over your solar plexus or stomach area and imagine the energy is traveling down through your legs and up into your neck and head. You can send your zero to yourself while sitting down also.

These days, I do the majority of my healing sessions for clients either at trade shows and events where the client must sit in a straight backed chair, or I do distance healing sessions at my office where I am also sitting in a chair. The massage table is great if you are a licensed massage therapist, but otherwise, it's not necessary, and can actually be cumbersome to carry around.

Since the primary numbers are delivered through the top of the head, you can always just work by sending energy there, and you don't need to have people lying down anymore.
There's no right or wrong way to do this and the process is simple. However you feel best delivering the energy is perfect.

I like that you do not have to come up with any weird representations for the symbols. We all know what numbers look like. How refreshing! Numbers are deeply embedded in our collective unconscious, so it's easy to do, and well received from your own Higher Self and other recipients. Next up, we'll talk about how to do this process for others.

# CHAPTER SIX
# HEALING OTHERS WITH PRIMARY NUMBERS

Once you've spent some time working on yourself and you feel like you're balanced and the best version of yourself you can be, then it's okay for you to expand and move on to assist others.

Using the primary numbers for healing is very easy to do and quite powerful as a tool for helping other people.

Begin the session by saying a prayer for the person's wellbeing. A great one I love to use is:

*You are free to accept or reject this healing. May Higher Will be done.*

Then begin sending the numbers 1 through 9 through the crown of their head.

Next, before you send the zero which is the final step, you can now begin to address any specific issues the person told you about or any areas where you intuitively believe more healing is needed. This is a good time to read the earlier material about what each number can do and work accordingly. Then again, you can also just open your own mind and imagination to receive whatever comes to you and know that is for the best.

When someone comes to me for healing, I assume they are probably stressed out to a certain extent and they need to get outside of themselves and feel a peaceful release from reality.

Because of that, the first number I send is the number 1. This number is about peace, wholeness, unity and feeling okay within yourself, knowing that we are all one in the same and that separateness is an illusion.

While the person is either sitting in the chair with you or lying on the massage table, just put your hand over their energy field and imagine seeing or feeling the energy of the number one flowing from your hand. You can strengthen this feeling by imagining the one is a purplish-violet color or just see the violet light moving into the energy field.

Next, because I think the heart center is the most important part of each of us,

I would move next to the number seven which heals the heart. Many people have broken hearts both physically and energetically. Maybe it is an actual heart condition, or maybe it is more of an emotional nature caused by heartache or grief. Regardless of what it is, it is always important to work to heal the heart because from there, lots of wonderful things will happen.

To do this, see the pink color – it could be a light baby pink, or a darker hot pink. See the number seven and send it right into the person's heart. Imagine the pink color and the seven energy expands now to move throughout the person's energy field.

What you are doing here is allowing the visual image of the number seven to represent a healing heart, love and understanding.

You will usually want to talk to someone about what they need to see you for prior to beginning the healing session. At this time, you may find the client wants to attract new love. If this is the case, allow the pink seven energy to move thorough the energy field of the person and imagine that this energy is healing them and allowing them to vibrate at the appropriate frequency to bring in the person who is for their highest good.

Likewise, if they are healing from a relationship, imagine the pink light and seven energy is mending their heart back into wholeness and perfection. Whatever it is they need, allow the heart energy to work its wonders on them.

Next, since many people need a healing for healings sake, send the 3 next and imagine the green healing energies flowing to the person and relieving any physical ailments, while strengthening the immune system and revitalizing cells and organs.

The number three and the green energy is more for healing on the physical level, where the seven is more on the emotional level.

Send the peaceful green light and energy to the person and see them as healthy and whole. Hold your hands closer to the body, about an inch away, because this is the part of the Etheric field that affects physical well being.

Once healing has occurred on emotional and physical levels and a feeling of peace is restored through the violet light, I would recommend sending the number 5 next for energy. Lots of people I've worked on through the years need healing because they want more energy.

You know there are lots of stories in the news about the fact that we as a society are not getting enough sleep and rest these days – not nearly what the body actually needs. The five energy and the beautiful refreshing blue color will help the person feel rested, relaxed, yet energized to take on the day.

Send the five starting at the bottoms of the feet and imagine it is sweeping with an upward motion toward the crown of the head, lifting, energizing and cleansing the person from head to toe. Imagine them feeling refreshed and newly charged, ready for whatever the world has in store for them.

Next, give the person a dose of creative energy by sending the number six. In many of my earlier books, I described the energetic layers of a person and the creative energies, in my experience, are best delivered to the mental layer of the energetic field. This is the part of the subtle energy system that is directly linked with creativity and productivity so when you send the number six, I want you to imagine you are sending it to the energetic layers that are about six to eight inches above the physical body. Send the six, see the orange color of it and imagine you notice how it travels up the body from the base of the person's spine and down through their legs. Imagine they are opened up to new creativity and mental activity as you send the six.

Next, I would send the number eight which represents infinity. You can imagine it sweeping over the causal or spiritual layer of the field, those aspects of the person that are most closely connected to the all that is. This layer begins about a foot away from the physical body. Visualize, if you can, the eight morphing into an infinity symbol and see it rotating over the field in a clockwise direction. Then shift and notice it in a counter clockwise direction. Then shift it back again and play with the energy a bit and see which one the client responds to better. You may also see the peaceful aqua colored light filling the energy field. Notice if you feel the client's energy becoming lighter than it was when you started.

Next, the number nine will symbolize completion. You have cleared the field with peace, strengthened the heart, remedied any physical conditions, energized and connected the person to their source and now you are complete. The nine will allow you to wrap up and fill in the gaps, so to speak, on anything else the person needs. That could be your prayer or intent for this section. Just ask that whatever was not addressed previously be healed or remedied at this time. Notice a shimmering silvery pearl colored light filling the field as the person becomes more peaceful than before.

See the nine floating into each one of the three layers of energy – astral, affecting the physical body, mental, and relating to the mental state or abundance, and causal, your connection to source energy. I've included a chart on the following page so you can have a visual to guide you.

Next, send a number 2 into the field as a protective shield of golden light pours through the energy centers and protects and preserves all the good things that happened with the healing session.

You could imagine a big number 2 moving over the field and sealing it off, or you could send the number 2 into the three layers of the energy field or into each of the seven chakras. Better yet,

Shelley A. Kaehr, Ph.D.

## *Three Layers of Energy that form the Etheric Field*

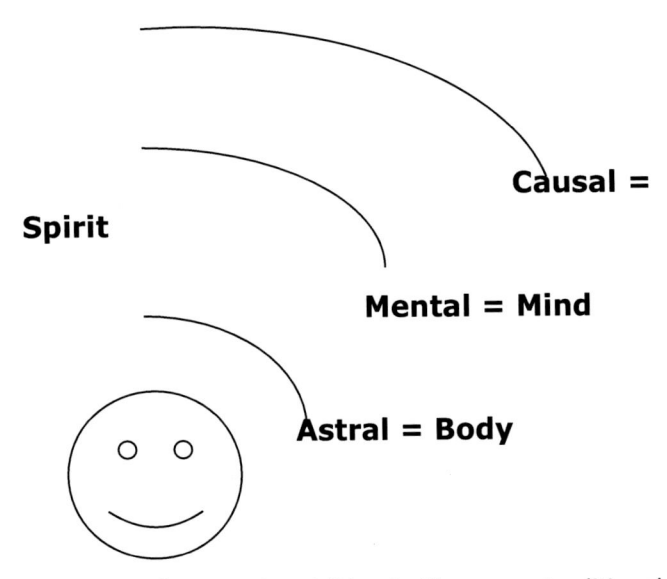

**Spirit**

**Causal = **

**Mental = Mind**

**Astral = Body**

*For your reference, in addition to the seven traditional colored chakra centers within the physical body, there is also an infinite field of light that surrounds you that is your true self, your soul, your energy body. In order to get our earthbound minds wrapped around how awesome we are, I often break up the field into different layers so we can discuss them easier in healing. The Astral layer relates to physical wellbeing, the Mental layer relates to mind and emotions and the Causal layer is spiritual and has to do with your karma and life lessons. You can see a lot more about these areas in my earlier books on gem and mineral healing.*

you could simply intend that all Primary Numbers are going exactly where they are needed for the highest good of the person receiving this energy and know that has been done and it is successful.

Next, you will send the red number four into each chakra center starting with the crown and moving down toward the feet. Imagine the client feeling grounded, centered and balanced. You may even like to talk them through the grounding by asking them to send any excess energy into their feet.

Send the four into the top of the head, the forehead, the throat, heart, and stomach, base of the spine, into the knees, ankles and feet and say something like this:

*"Bring excess energies down from your head, through your neck, shoulders, into your stomach, to the base of your spine, into your knees, ankles and out the soles of your feet and allow the energy to go down, down, down, into the earth. You are now grounded, centered and balanced."*

By doing this verbally while you are sending the 4 and the color red, you are allowing the person to take a more active role in their own healing and responsibility for grounding themselves. It works!

Finally, send the zero by imagining the golden circle of light is moving from the top of the person's head to their feet and continue imagining it moving up and down over their field until you are guided that they are complete. Intend that the healing continue to benefit the person and that they are grounded, centered and balanced. Bring your hands to prayer position and say a silent prayer for their wellbeing. I like to say this one:

*"Please allow this healing to continue."*

Bring your hands to prayer position and close your healing. Now that your session is over, ask the person to take their time coming to and to sit up whenever they feel comfortable and are ready to do so.

When they get up, if they are still dizzy, use the red number four again to ground them. Imagine the 4 moves down their energetic field while they are in a seated position, sending the 4 from the head to the feet while talking them once more about sending all excess energies into the ground.

That should work most of the time! If the person needs more, repeat as often as needed until they let you know they're grounded.

Remember that all people and sessions are unique so this is only a rough outline of one example of how you can use the individual numbers. If you have different feelings about the order of things, or you feel that the person may not need one of the numbers, then always follow your instincts! You know more than you give yourself credit for! I really want you to trust yourself and follow what your inner guidance tells you to do above all.

One main point I must add here is that initially when sending the numbers, you always do so through the top or crown of the head first and that results in the inner, cellular work being done.

Once that's been completed, you go through a second time and that's when the numbers can either be sent through the crown into the interior of the body, or as mentioned, you would then use the numbers for further clearing of the energy fields around the body. The result is a complete healing of body, mind and spirit!

Next, let's take a look at how to send somebody a distance healing.

# CHAPTER SEVEN
# DISTANCE HEALING
# WITH PRIMARY NUMBERS

Distance healing is easy with the Primary Number technique. Sit in a chair or special space where you won't be distracted. Visualize the person in your mind. If you know what they look like, awesome, if not, simply invite their Higher Self to join you.

Begin the session the same way you would for an in person healing by saying a prayer for the person's wellbeing:

*You are free to accept or reject this healing. May Higher Will be done.*

Next, visualize the person's head in front of you and send each of the numbers to them through the crown chakra, or top of their head, in this order:

**1-Peace**
**2-Protection**
**3-Healing**
**4-Grounding**
**5-Energy**
**6-Creativity**
**7-Heart**
**8-Infinity**
**9-Completion**

Once the first nine numbers have been sent, you're your imagination to surround the recipient's head with the golden zero and envision the zero moving from the top of the head to the soles of the feet, surrounding the body.

**0-Source**

Then per directions in the prior section, see what other areas need extra energy and work accordingly. Allow yourself to let go of preconceptions and just do what comes to you intuitively, the same way you would intuitively use any other healing method.

After sending all the numbers, end the healing when you no longer feel a huge rush of energy, or when you're guided to finish. Say a closing prayer aloud or to yourself: *"Please allow this healing to continue."*

Bring your hands to prayer position, wish the recipient the best, and know all is well. That's it! Super simple!

# CHAPTER EIGHT
# GROUP HEALING
# WITH PRIMARY NUMBERS

Group healing using the primary numbers is similar to any other energy exchange you've participated in.

Put one person in a chair or have them lay down on a massage table, depending on what you have available, and have all other group members surround them.

Each person in the group should silently say a prayer for the recipient's well being, or if you prefer, one person can say the prayer so everybody can hear:

*"You are free to accept or reject this healing. May Higher Will be done."*

Begin by sending all the numbers to the person receiving, including the zero. At the same time, each of your other healers will be doing the same.

In this scenario, you may not be standing near the recipient's head, so send the numbers into the body, wherever you can, or wherever you're guided.

Plan to send all the numbers to them, but always listen to the inner voice. When I participate in group healings, sometimes I am guided to only send one symbol because I know for a fact that other people will be sending the person all the symbols. For example, if you're getting that the person needs the number 4 and you sense this is your "job" so to speak, then send the 4 only and know all is well. Use your intuition above all else!

Allow the healing energies to flow until you're guided to stop. You may notice when the person is finished that many healers end the session at the same time. You may also notice the process goes faster with everyone sending the energy together.

End as usual with hands in prayer and wishing the person well. In the group setting you still want to at least think the phrase:

*"Please allow this healing to continue."*

Help the person up and then switch recipients and have each healer move to different places around the person so you can try healing from different angles.

Remember to tune in to what each person needs and how you're supposed to be delivering the energy. Repeat until everyone in your group has given and received a healing. Experiment and compare notes and provide feedback to each other when you're done.

That's it! Most important is to have fun! Why would I say that? Because the world needs happiness and if your heart's not in it, wait until it is!

## CONCLUSION

With all the technology and information that is readily available to us, time is speeding up. People need information quickly and easily. We don't need a ton of words. We need the information imparted as quickly as it can be transmitted. For these reasons, the *Pythagorean Healing* books will be designed for speed, simplicity and affordability.

Now that you've tried Pythagorean Healing Level One in the way I described, I'd like to conclude this short book by reminding you of something I have been talking about in every book I've written, and that is that you have the power and knowingness within you to do whatever you want to do. Trust your guidance! Always remember this is only a roadmap and you may discover a new way as you work with someone using this method and that's awesome!

Yes, we are all one, and yes we are all connected, but we are also each a unique manifestation of the life force, and because of that, everyone will respond differently to various healing methods. Always use your intuition. Go with the flow, trust yourself. Do what needs to be done for your friend or client, and especially for yourself. You have all the capabilities right now to do this. It's fun and easy!

I hope working with Pythagorean Healing and the primary numbers will bring you and yours much peace and be of help to you on your path. Stay tuned for the next technique in this new series. Meanwhile, know I am always cheering you on from the sidelines! Namaste!

## WEBSITE RESOURCES

**Numerology Calculator** – I suggest Googling this term and seeing which one resonates best with you. Explore the numbers as they relate to your own name, birthday, etc.

**Pythagoras**
https://www.ancient.eu/Pythagoras/

**Transporter from Star Trek** Want to see the transporters at work in the various incarnations of Star Trek?
https://en.wikipedia.org/wiki/Transporter_(Star_Trek)
Check out this video!
https://www.youtube.com/watch?v=Oxh-qoLz_pM

# ABOUT THE AUTHOR

Shelley Kaehr, Ph.D. is known as one of the world's leading authorities on energy healing and mind-body medicine. She developed several energy healing methods including Edgar Cayce's Egyptian Energy Healing, Holographic Mapping and the new Pythagorean Healing Method and is widely known as an expert on the healing properties of gems and minerals.

Her work as a past life regressionist has been endorsed by Dr. Brian Weiss who calls her work, "An important contribution to the field of regression therapy."

Visit Shelley online:
www.pastlifelady.com
Join the Discussion on Shelley's social media:
Facebook Fan Pages: Past Life Lady, Shelley Kaehr
YouTube: Past Life Lady
Instagram: shelleykaehr
Twitter: @ShelleyKaehr

Made in the USA
Monee, IL
13 August 2020